# HISTORIC STYLES
## STAINED GLASS PATTERN BOOK

83 Designs for Workable Projects

by

Ed Sibbett, Jr.

DOVER PUBLICATIONS, INC., NEW YORK

Published in Canada by General Publishing Company, Ltd., 30 Lesmill Road, Don Mills, Toronto, Ontario.
Published in the United Kingdom by Constable and Company, Ltd.

*Historic Styles Stained Glass Pattern Book: 83 Designs for Workable Projects* is a new work, first published by Dover Publications, Inc., in 1981.

DOVER *Pictorial Archive* SERIES

*International Standard Book Number: 0-486-24176-9*
*Library of Congress Catalog Card Number: 81-67089*

Manufactured in the United States of America
Dover Publications, Inc.
31 East 2nd Street
Mineola, N.Y. 11501

# PUBLISHER'S NOTE

One of the glories of stained glass is its limitless adaptability to any style of design. In this volume, Ed Sibbett, Jr., has created 83 stained glass patterns, using as his inspiration a wide variety of historic sources, ranging from Egyptian motifs such as the scarab to the attractive geometric play of Art Deco. Some of the other styles represented are the elaborate interlaced beasts of Celtic art, the winning designs of the Pennsylvania Dutch and the graceful motifs of the Orient. The patterns can be adapted to a wide variety of craft projects—windows, lampshades, mirrors, ornaments, mobiles, etc. Suppliers of glass and other materials, including general instruction books and tools for the beginner, should be listed in your local Yellow Pages.

# CONTENTS

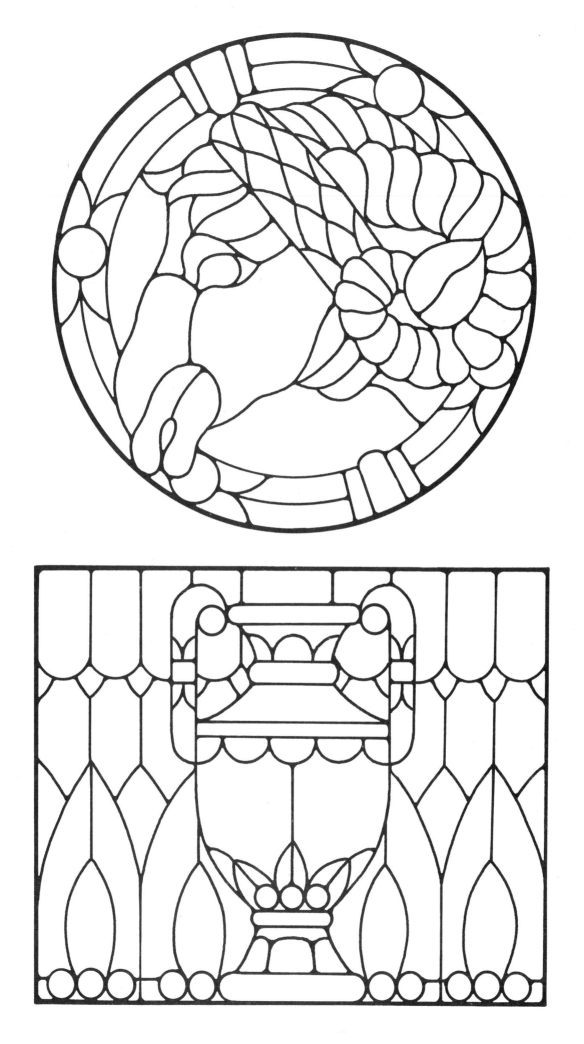

3

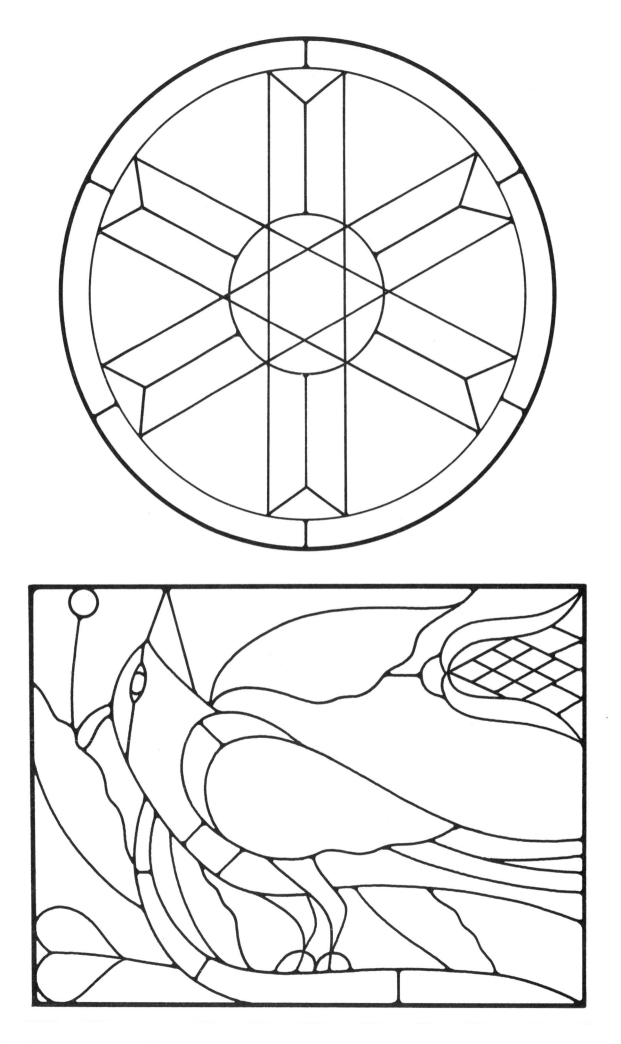

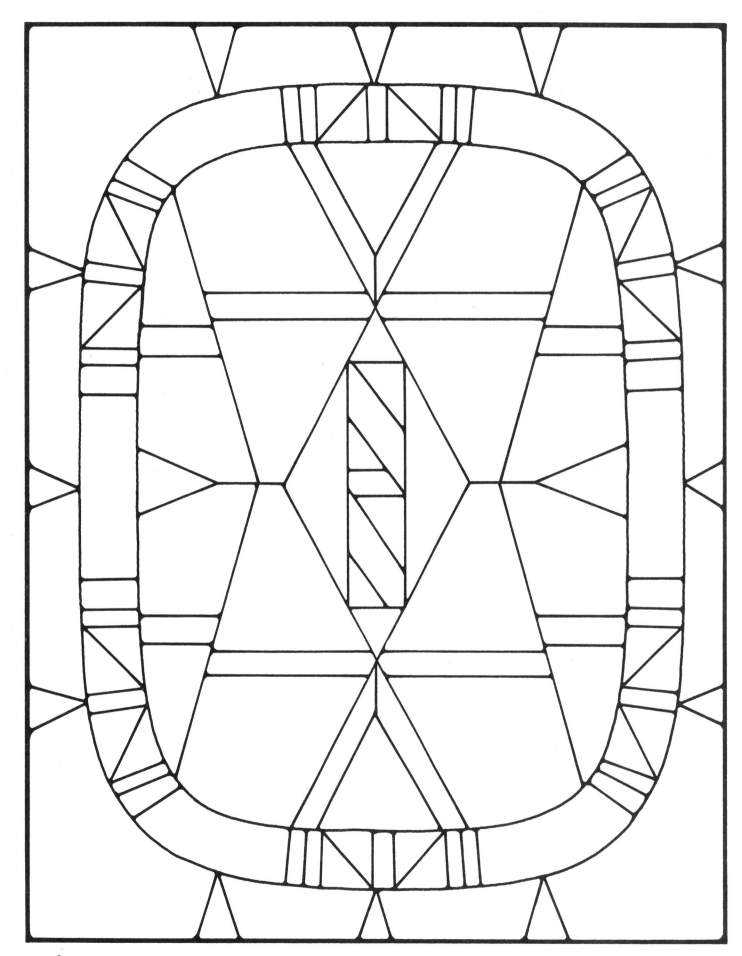

6

7

9

11

12

14

17

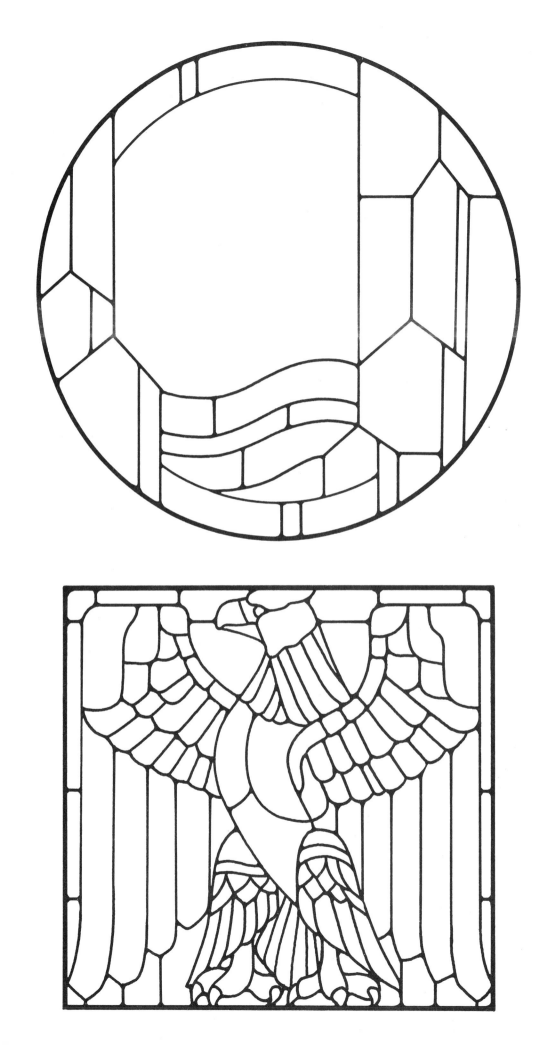

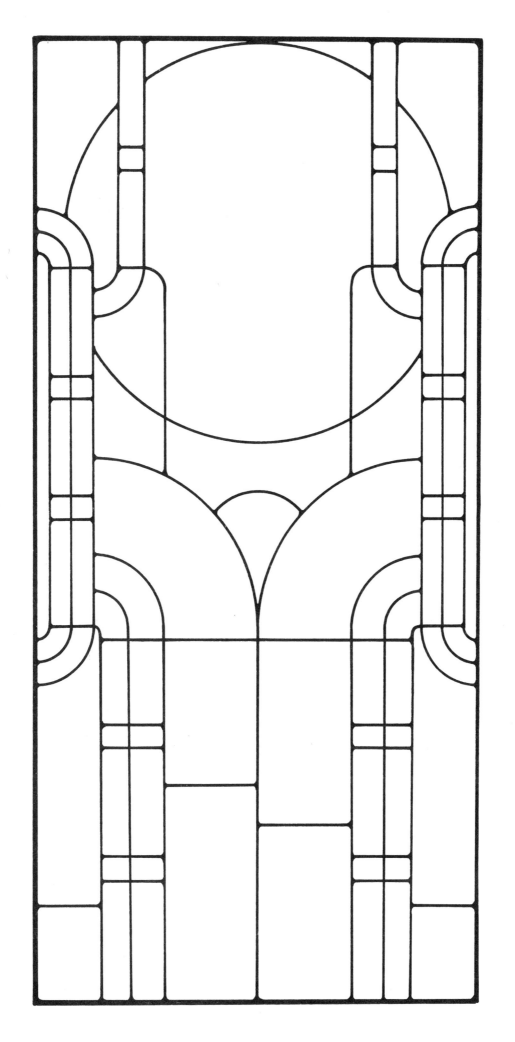

19

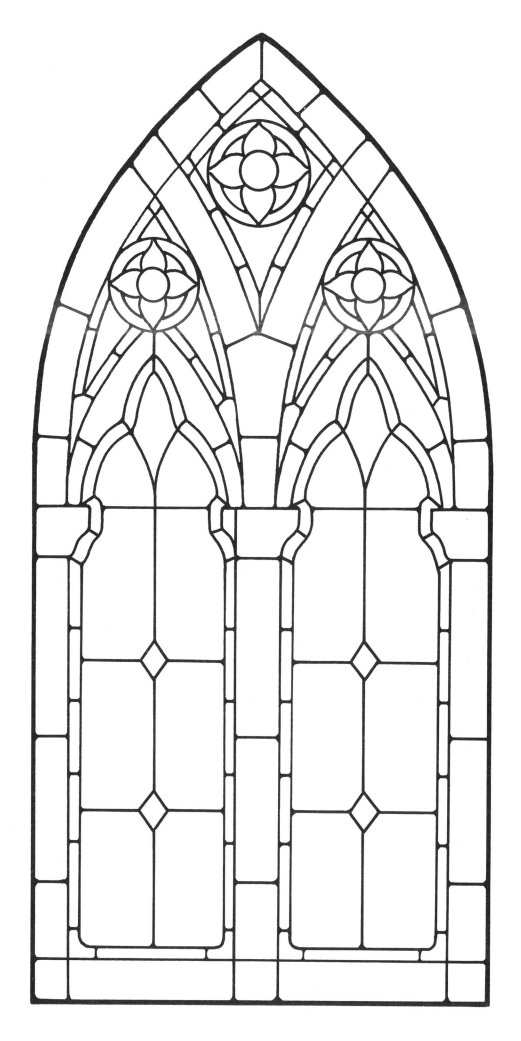

24

33

34

39

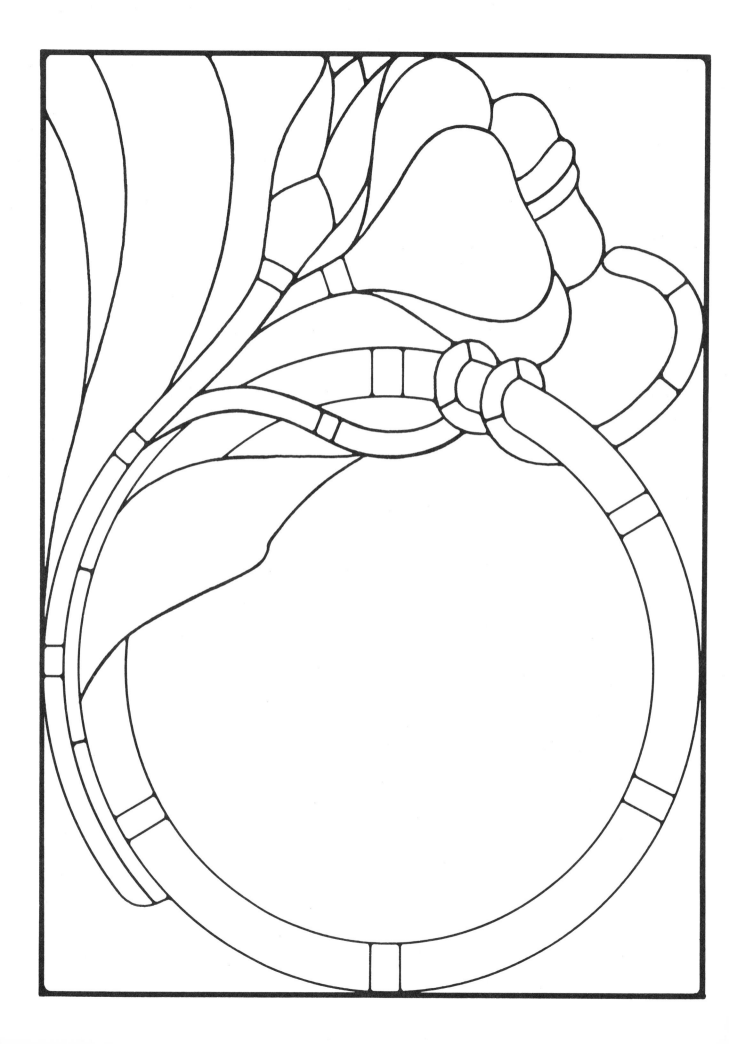

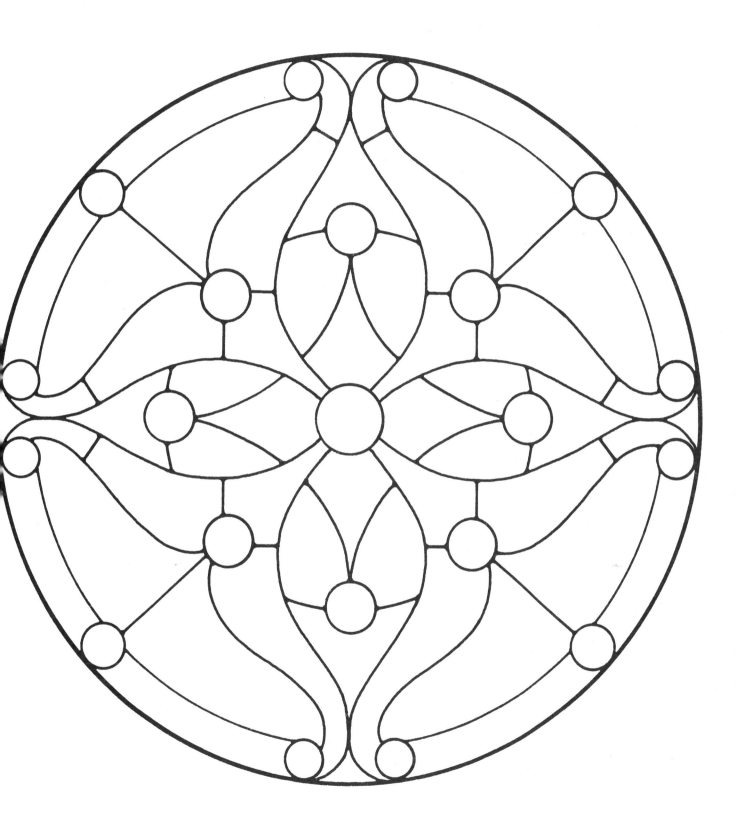

46

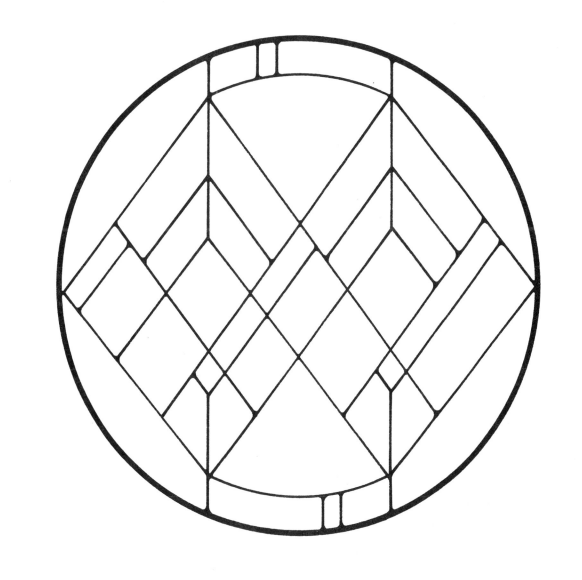

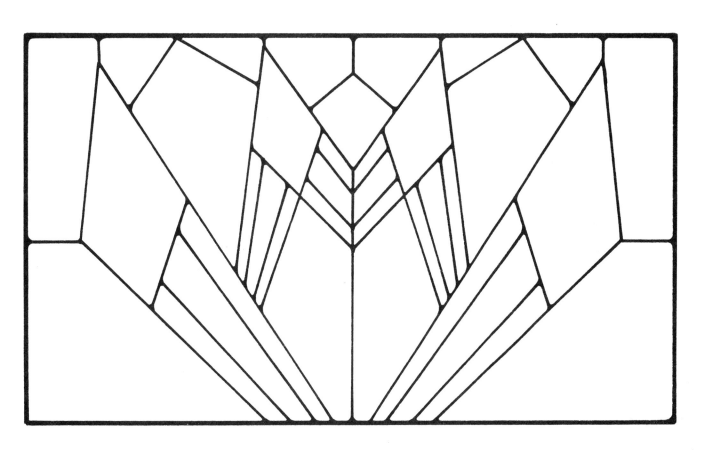

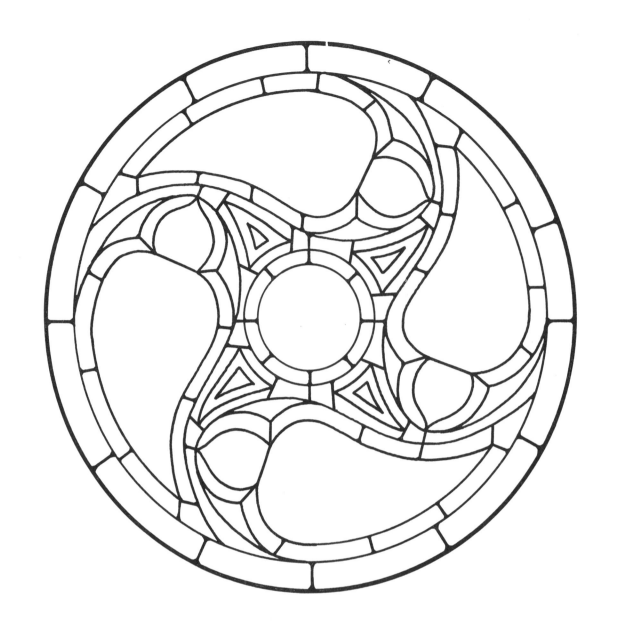

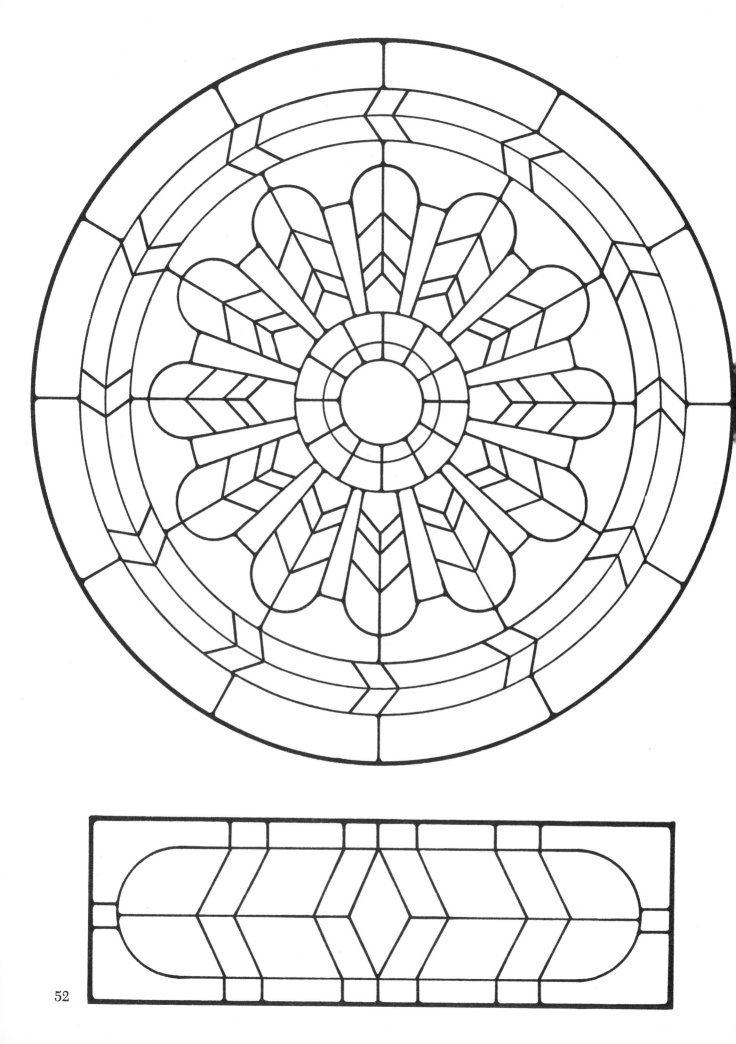

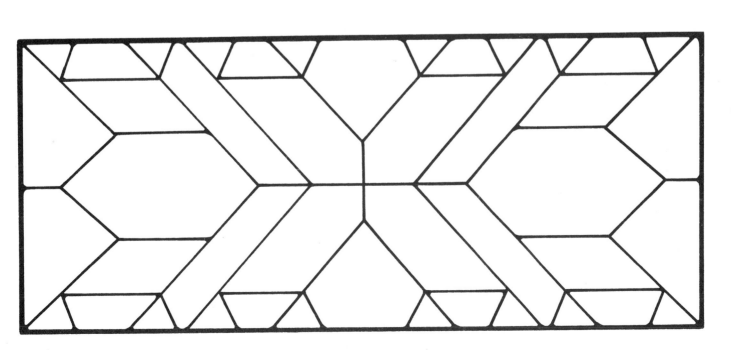

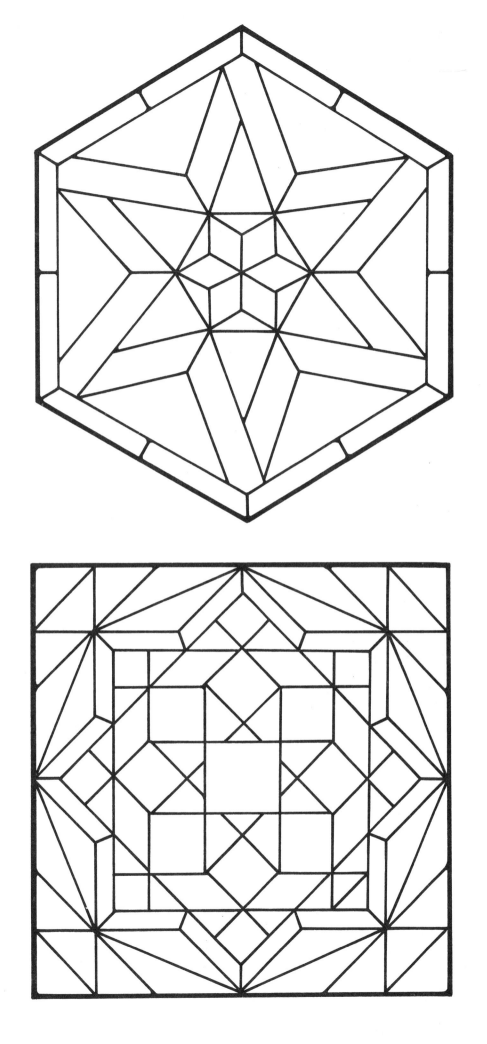